STARS OF THE
BALLET
AND
DANCE

in Performance Photographs

by

FRED FEHL

With best wishes
Fred Fehl

DOVER PUBLICATIONS, INC.
NEW YORK

To my dear wife Margaret,
my constant companion at the ballet

Books with Performance Photographs
by Fred Fehl

Pas de Deux: The Art of Partnering, by Anton Dolin, 1949, Kamin Dance Publishers, New York. (Dover reprint 22038-9.)

Melissa Hayden On Stage and Off, by M. Hayden, 1963, Doubleday, Garden City, New York.

Beyond Technique, by Erik Bruhn, 1968, Dance Perspectives, New York.

On Broadway, text by William Stott with Jane Stott, 1978, University of Texas Press, Austin.

Giselle and Albrecht, text by Doris Hering, 1981, Dance Horizons, New York.

The New York City Opera Sings, 1981, New York City Opera Guild, New York.

The New York City Opera, by Martin Sokol, 1981, Macmillan, New York.

Stars of the Broadway Stage 1940–1967 in Performance Photographs, 1983, Dover Publications, Inc., New York.

For the past forty years Fred Fehl's photographs on dance, theater and music have been published in hundreds of magazines and countless books in the United States as well as in Europe.

Published in Canada by General Publishing Company, Ltd., 30 Lesmill Road, Don Mills, Toronto, Ontario.

Published in the United Kingdom by Constable and Company, Ltd., 10 Orange Street, London WC2H 7EG.

Stars of the Ballet and Dance in Performance Photographs is a new work, first published by Dover Publications, Inc., in 1984.

Manufactured in the United States of America
Dover Publications, Inc., 32 East 2nd Street, Mineola, N.Y. 11501

Library of Congress Cataloging in Publication Data

Fehl, Fred.
Stars of the ballet and dance in performance photographs.

Includes index.
1. Dancing—Pictorial works.   2. Ballet—Pictorial works.   3. Dancers—Pictorial works.   4. Ballet dancers—Pictorial works.   I. Title.
GV1596.F44   1983   793.3   82-18294
ISBN 0-486-24492-X

Fred Fehl. *(Photo by Hans Geiger)*

About the Author

Fred Fehl was born and raised in Vienna, one of the major cultural centers of Europe. From his father, a prominent dentist, he inherited not only his love of theater and music, but also his interest in photography. To escape the Nazis he had to flee Vienna in 1938. Coming to America he combined his two great hobbies and became a theatrical photographer.

Since 1940 he has photographed over 60 ballet and dance companies, among them the American Ballet Theatre, the New York City Ballet, the Ballet Russe de Monte Carlo, the Robert Joffrey Ballet, Martha Graham and Dance Company, the Alvin Ailey City Center Theater.

From 1940 to 1970 he photographed nearly 1,000 Broadway and Off-Broadway productions. He photographed the New York City Opera from 1944 to 1980 and has also captured images of many classical musicians.

Fehl says: "To me ballet is the most fascinating and beautiful movement of the human body that can be captured by the camera. I photograph various aspects of the performing arts, but nothing is as gratifying to me as classical ballet. And I always prefer photographing during performance, because a performance alone offers the flow of movement as well as the artists' highest emotional expression. Of course two things are all-important. First, one must be an expert photographer and, second, one must have a keen sense and understanding of dance movement. The most interesting experience for me is showing these action photographs to the artists and watching their amazement, surprise, enthusiasm—or, sometimes, disappointment when they see that they did

something wrong, for the pictures show them as the audience saw them. Choreographers who dance in their own ballets will frequently notice some step they wish they had not done and make corrections for the next performance."

Fehl's photographs have appeared in hundreds of books, among them *The American Ballet Theatre* by Charles Payne and *40 Years of New York City Ballet* by Nancy Reynolds, each one with nearly 100 of his photographs. In *Erik Bruhn: Danseur Noble*, by John Gruen, the majority of photographs are by Fehl. During the past 40 years Fehl has contributed photographs to *Life, Look, Time, Newsweek, Vogue, the New York Times, This Week, Glamour, Ladies Home Journal, Dance, Theatre Arts, Dance News, Dancing Times, Ballet News, Dance and Dancers, Madame, Ballet Annual* and others.

In 1976, 450 of Fehl's photographs of dance, theater, the New York City Opera and classical musicians were exhibited at the Lincoln Center Library for the Performing Arts under the title *Fred Fehl: Photographer of the Performing Arts*. The exhibit was so popular that it was extended three times and ran for seven and a half months. Earlier exhibits of his work were held at Columbia University, the Philadelphia Art Alliance, the University of Ohio, the Art Gallery at the New York City Center and others.

Photographs of the American Ballet Theatre and the New York City Ballet are not included in this book. Two books, one on each company, will be published by Dover Publications in the future.

Contents

All numbers are those of the illustrations.

1–26. Television Productions. 1. *Apollo* (1963). Melissa Hayden, Jacques D'Amboise.

2

2. *Coppélia* (1963). Erik Bruhn.
3. *Coppélia* (1963). Erik Bruhn,
Sonia Arova.

3

4. *Flower Festival* (1962). Rudolf Nureyev. 5. *Flower Festival* (1962). Rudolf Nureyev, Maria Tallchief.

6

7

6. *Flower Festival* (1962). Rudolf Nureyev. 7. *Le Corsaire* (1962). Rudolf Nureyev. 8. *Le Corsaire* (in rehearsal; 1962). Rudolf Nureyev.

4

10

11

9, 10. *Romeo and Juliet* (1967). Erik Bruhn, Carla Fracci. 11. *Romeo and Juliet* (1967). Erik Bruhn.

12, 13. *Swan Lake* (Black Swan Pas de Deux; 1963). Erik Bruhn, Sonia Arova.

14

15

10

14, 15. *Swan Lake* (Black Swan Pas de Deux; 1963). Erik Bruhn, Sonia Arova. 16, 17. *Swan Lake* (1965). Margot Fonteyn, Rudolf Nureyev.

18, 19. *Swan Lake* (1965). Margot Fonteyn, Rudolf Nureyev. 20. *Swan Lake* (1965). Margot Fonteyn.

21
22

21, 22. *Swan Lake* (1965). Margot Fonteyn, Rudolf
Nureyev. 23, 24. *La Sylphide* (1963). Erik Bruhn,
Carla Fracci.

24

25. *La Sylphide* (1963). Erik Bruhn. 26. *La Sylphide*. Erik Bruhn, Carla Fracci.

27–40. Alvin Ailey City Center Dance Theater. 27. *After Eden* (1975). Sara Yarborough, Christopher Aponte.

30

28. *Choros* (1972). Sara Yarborough. 29. *Carmina Burana* (1973). Sara Yarborough, Michihiko Oka, Judith Jamison, John Parks. 30. *Cry* (1972). Judith Jamison.

31. *Flowers* (1971). Lynn Seymour, Ramon Segara. 32, 33. *Flowers* (1971). Lynn Seymour. 34. *Mary Lou's Mass* (1972). Sara Yarborough, John Parks. 35. *Icarus* (1969). Dudley Williams, Consuelo Atlas.

36, 37. *Pas de Duke* (1976). Mikhail Baryshnikov. 38. *Pas de Duke* (1976). Judith Jamison, Mikhail Baryshnikov.

39

39. *Rainbow 'Round My Shoulder* (1972). Sara Yarborough, Dudley Williams. 40. *Portrait of Billie* (1975). Sara Yarborough. **41–43. The American Dance Theatre.** *A Choreographic Offering* (1964). José Limon.

40

24

41

43

44, 45. Antonio and the Ballets de Madrid (1968). 44. Rosario. 45. Antonio. **46, 47. Argentinita** (1942). 46. With José Greco.

26

48

48. **The Australian Ballet.** *Don Quixote* (1971). Rudolf Nureyev.

50

49–52. Ballet of the 20th Century (Maurice Béjart). 49.
Bhakti (1971). Paolo Bortoluzzi, unidentified dancer. 50.
Nomos Alpha (1971). Paolo Bortoluzzi. 51. *Firebird*
(1971). Paolo Bortoluzzi.

29

52. *Les Fleurs du Mal* (1971). Suzanne Farrell, Jorge Donn.

53. Ballet Rambert. *Giselle* (1959; U.S. debut at Jacob's Pillow). Beryl Goldwyn.

54–79. Ballet Russe de Monte Carlo. 54. *Baiser de la Fée* (1940s). Alexandra Danilova. 55. *Le Beau Danube* (1942). Alexandra Danilova, Léonide Massine. 56. *Coppélia* (1949). Alexandra Danilova. 57. *Coppélia* (1949). Michel Katcharoff, Alexandra Danilova.

57

58

59

58. *Gaîté Parisienne* (1942). Léonide Massine. 59. *Gaîté Parisienne* (1940s). Frederic Franklin, Alexandra Danilova.

60. *Raymonda* (1948). Alexandra Danilova, Frederic Franklin. 61. *Rodeo* (1944). Casimir Kokitch, Agnes DeMille, Frederic Franklin. 62 (overleaf). *Pas de Quatre* (1948). Mia Slavenska, Alicia Markova, Alexandra Danilova, Nathalie Krassovska.

65

63. *Giselle* (1949). Alexandra Danilova, Frederic Franklin. 64. *Giselle* (1949). Anton Dolin, Alicia Markova. 65. *Giselle* (1948). Mia Slavenska. 66. *Giselle* (1940s). Tamara Toumanova, Anton Dolin.

66

67. *Giselle* (1948). Mia Slavenska.
68. *Nutcracker* (1948). Alexandra Danilova, Frederic Franklin. 69. *Nutcracker* (1948). Leon Danielian. 70. *Nutcracker* (1948). Mary Ellen Moylan, Oleg Tupine.

69

70

71

71. *Nutcracker* (1948). Alicia Markova, Anton Dolin.

72

73

74

72. *Swan Lake* (1948). Mia Slavenska,
Anton Dolin. 73. *Swan Lake* (1940s).
Tamara Toumanova. 74. *Swan Lake*
(1949). Frederic Franklin, Alexandra
Danilova. 75. *Seventh Symphony*
(1948). Alicia Markova, Anton Dolin.
76. *Snow Maiden* (1942). Alexandra
Danilova.

76

77

77. *Variations for Three* (1940s). André Eglevsky, Rosella Hightower, Anton Dolin. 78. *Scheherazade* (1942). Mia Slavenska. 79. *Scheherazade* (1949). Alexandra Danilova.

78

80

80. Fred Berk Repertory Dance Co. (1950s). Fred Berk, Katja Delakova.

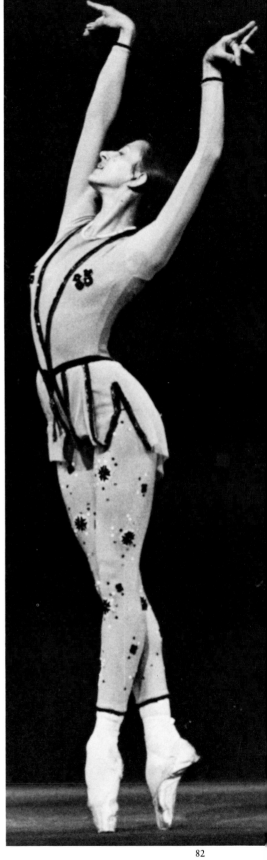

81

82

81–90. Bolshoi Ballet. 81. *The Legend of Love* (1979). Alexander
Bogatyrev. 82. *The Legend of Love* (1979). Natalia Bessmertnova.

49

83

83. *Romeo and Juliet* (1979). Vyacheslav Gordeyev, Nadezhda Pavlova.

84

85

84, 85. *Romeo and Juliet* (1979). Nadezhda Pavlova.

86. *Nutcracker* (1969). Vladimir Vasiliev. 87. *Nutcracker* (1969). Ekaterina Maximova, Vladimir Vasiliev. 88. *Spartacus* (1979). Nadezhda Pavlova, Vyacheslav Gordeyev.

89. *Spartacus* (1979). Vyacheslav
Gordeyev. 90. *Spartacus* (1979).
Vyacheslav Gordeyev, Nadezhda
Pavlova.

91, 92. Berlin Opera Ballet. 91. *Le Corsaire* (Pas de Deux; 1978). Valerii Panov, Galina Panova. 92. *Daphnis and Chloe* (1978). Eva Evdokimova, Reda Sheta.

93

93, 94. Valerie Bettis Dance Theatre. 93. *As I Lay Dying* (1949). Valerie Bettis. **94.** *As I Lay Dying*
(1949). Valerie Bettis, Duncan Noble. **95. John Butler Dance Theatre.** *The Brass World* (1954). Glen
Tetley, Carmen Guttierev, Felisia Conde.

96–98. Merce Cunningham and Dance Company. 96. *The Monkey Dances* (1950s). Merce Cunningham. 97. *Scramble* (1970). Carolyn Brown, Merce Cunningham. 98. *Scramble* (1970). Merce Cunningham.

98

99

101

102

99–110. Dance Gala, March 24, 1972. 99. *Sleeping Beauty* (Grand Pas de Deux, Act III). Margot Fonteyn. **100–102.** *Sleeping Beauty* (Grand Pas de Deux, Act III). Margot Fonteyn, Attilio Labis.

103

104

103. *Don Quixote* (Pas de Deux). Helgi Tomasson. 104, 105. *Don Quixote* (Pas de Deux). Gelsey Kirkland.

106. *Don Quixote* (Pas de Deux). Gelsey Kirkland, Helgi Tomasson. 107. *Pas de Deux*. Melissa Hayden, Peter Martins. 108. *Pas de Deux*. Peter Martins.

109

109. *Pas de Quatre*. Violette Verdy, Patricia McBride, Carla Fracci, Eleanor D'Antuono. 110. Curtain Call. Front row, left to right: Eleanor D'Antuono, Agnes DeMille, Margot Fonteyn, Carla Fracci, Melissa Hayden, Judith Jamison, Maria Karnilova, Gelsey Kirkland, Natalia Makarova. Second row, left to right: Merce Cunningham, Leon Danielian, Anton Dolin, John Kriza, Attilio Labis, Peter Martins, Lawrence Rhodes, Helgi Tomasson.

111

112

111, 112. Carmen de Lavallade. *Ballet Ballads* (1961). Carmen de Lavallade.
113, 114. Chicago Opera Ballet. *Don Quixote* (Pas de Deux, 1962). Rudolf
Nureyev, Sonia Arova.

115. Gagaku (1959).

116

117

116–121. Katherine Dunham and Her Dance Company (1945).
Katherine Dunham.

118

122

123

122–124. Lotte Goslar. *Clowns and Other Fools* (1966). Lotte Goslar.

124

125–147. Martha Graham and Dance Company. 125.
Cave of the Heart (1968). Robert Cohan, Takako
Asakawa, Noemi Lapzeson. 126. *Canticle for Innocent Comedians* (1969). Noemi Lapzeson.

126

127. *Dark Meadow* (1969). Martha Graham, Matt Turney. 128. *Cortege of Eagles* (1968). Martha Graham. 129. *Cortege of Eagles* (1968). Robert Powell, Martha Graham, Moss Cohen.

128

129

130

131

130. *The Lady of the House of Sleep* (1968). Martha Graham. 131. *The Lady of the House of Sleep* (1968). William Louther, Martha Graham, Bertram Ross. 132, 133. *Night Journey* (1968). Ethel Winter, Bertram Ross.

134. *Night Journey* (1940). Martha Graham. 135. *Stephen Acrobat* (1947). Erick Hawkins, Stuart Hodes. 136. *A Time of Snow* (1968). Bertram Ross, Martha Graham. 137. *A Time of Snow* (1968). Martha Graham.

135

136

137

138

138. *Phaedra* (1969). Robert Cohan,
Takako Asakawa, Bertram Ross. 139.
The Plain of Prayer (1968). Takako
Asakawa, Robert Powell. 140, 141.
El Penitente (1943). Erick Hawkins,
Pearl Lang.

139

142. *Letter to the World* (1947). Martha Graham. 143. *Letter to the World* (1947). Jean Erdman, Martha Graham. 144. *Letter to the World* (1947). Martha Graham.

145
146

147

145. *Punch and the Judy* (1940s). Robert Cohan, Martha Graham, Stuart Hodes, Mark Ryder. 146, 147. *Punch and the Judy* (1940s). Martha Graham, Robert Cohan. **148–158. Harkness Ballet.** 148. *Feast of Ashes* (1967). Brunilda Ruiz, Salvatore Aiello. 149. *Canto Indio* (1969). Helgi Tomasson, Elisabeth Carroll.

149

150

150. *Sylvia* (Pas de Deux; 1969). Elisabeth Carroll, Helgi Tomasson. 151. *Grand Pas Espagnol* (1969). Marina Eglevsky, Lone Isaksen, Elisabeth Carroll, Finis Jhung, Lawrence Rhodes, Helgi Tomasson. 152. *Le Diable à Quatre* (1969). Helgi Tomasson. 153. *Le Diable à Quatre* (1969). Lawrence Rhodes.

154

154. *Firebird* (1967). Elisabeth Carroll. 155. *Monument for a Dead Boy* (1969). Lawrence Rhodes, Dennis Wayne. 156. *Monument for a Dead Boy* (1969). Lone Isaksen, Lawrence Rhodes.

157

157. *Variations for Four Plus Four* (1967). Finis Jhung.

158. *Variations for Four Plus Four* (1967). Lawrence Rhodes, unidentified dancer.

159
160

159. Humphry-Weidman Company. *And Daddy Was a Fireman* (1943). Charles Weidman. **160–176. Robert Joffrey Ballet.** 160. *The Green Table* (1967). Maximiliano Zomosa, Lisa Bradley. 161. *The Green Table* (1967). Michael Uthoff. 162. *Astarte* (1968). Trinette Singleton, Maximiliano Zomosa.

162

95

163

164

163. *Cakewalk* (1968). Gary Chryst. 164. *Cakewalk* (1968). Maximiliano Zomosa, Barbara Remington. 165. *Nightwings* (1967). Lisa Bradley, Michael Uthoff. 166. *Petrouchka* (1970). Dermot Burke, Erika Goodman, Gary Chryst.

166

167

168

169

167. *Pas de Déesses* (1968). Brunilda Ruiz, Michael Uthoff. 168. *Pas de Déesses* (1968). Sally Brailey, Michael Uthoff. 169. *Pas de Déesses* (1969). Charthel Arthur, Barbara Remington, Burton Taylor, Susan Magno. 170. *Pas de Déesses* (1967). Lisa Bradley. 171. *Pas de Déesses* (1967). Noel Mason.

98

172

173

100

174

175

176

172. *Façade* (1969). Trinette Singleton, Edward Verso. 173. *Three-Cornered Hat* (1969). Barbara Remington, Luis Fuente. 174. *Scotch Symphony* (1968). Sally Brailey. 175. *Sea Shadow* (1968). Lisa Bradley, Paul Sutherland. 176. *William Tell Variation* (1969). Bill Martin-Viscount.

177. **Jooss Ballet.** *Drums Sound in Hackensack* (1941). Ulla Soederbaum. **178. Esther Junger** (1940s).

179. Kabuki (1969). **180. Pearl Lang Company.** *Shira* (1969). Pearl Lang.

180

182

181

181–183. Marcel Marceau (1975).

183

184. Nala Najan. *Dances of India* (1966).

185

185–188. National Ballet of Canada. 185, 186. *Swan Lake* (1967). Erik Bruhn, Lois Smith. 187. *Coppélia* (1979). Rudolf Nureyev, Veronica Tennant. 188. *Coppélia* (1979). Erik Bruhn, Rudolf Nureyev.

186

189, 190. National Ballet of Washington. 189. *Idylle Pas de Deux* (1967). Ivan Nagy, Marilyn Burr. **190.** *Les Sylphides* (1967).
Ivan Nagy, Jane Miller. **191–195. New York City Opera. 191.** *Le Bourgeois Gentilhomme* (1979). Rudolf Nureyev.

192

193

194

195

192. *Le Bourgeois Gentilhomme* (1979). Rudolf Nureyev. 193.
Le Bourgeois Gentilhomme (1979). Patricia McBride, Rudolf
Nureyev. 194, 195. *Le Bourgeois Gentilhomme* (1979). Rudolf
Nureyev. **196, 197. Alwin Nikolais Dance Theatre. 196.** *Ten-*
sile Involvement from Masks, Props and Mobiles (1969). 197
(overleaf). *Imago* (1969).

198–208. Original Ballet Russe. 198. *Aurora's Wedding* (1940). Tatiana Ria-bouchinska, David Lichine. 199. *Balustrade* (1941). Tatiana Leskova, Roman Jasinsky, Tamara Toumanova, Paul Petroff, Marina Svetlova. 200. *Don Quix-ote* (Grand Pas de Deux; 1946). Rosella Hightower, Georges Skibine. 201. *Don Quixote* (Grand Pas de Deux; 1946). Rosella Hightower.

202

203

202. *Paganini* (1946). Vladimir Dokoudovsky. 203. *Les Sylphides* (1940). Tatiana Riabouchinska. 204. *Coq d'Or* (1940). Tatiana Riabouchinska. 205. *Coq d'Or* (1940). Irina Baronova.

208

206. *Francesca da Rimini* (1946). Lubov Tchernicheva. 207. *Camille* (1946). Alicia Markova, Anton Dolin. 208. *Camille* (1946). Alicia Markova.

209. Pennsylvania Ballet. *Carmina Burana* (1968). Fiona Fuerstner, Ross Parkes.
210–223. Royal Danish Ballet. 210. *The Lesson* (1965). Henning Kronstam, Mette Honningen. 211. *Miss Julie* (1965). Erik Bruhn, Kirsten Simone.

212
213

214

212. *La Sylphide* (1965). Flemming
Flindt, Margrethe Schanne. 213. *La
Sylphide* (1965). Margrethe Schanne.
214. *La Sylphide* (1965). Margrethe
Schanne, Flemming Flindt. 215. *La Syl-
phide* (1965). Kirsten Simone, Erik
Bruhn. 216. *La Sylphide* (1965). Niels
Bjørn Larsen, Erik Bruhn.

217

218

219

217–219. *Carmen* (1965). Kirsten Simone, Erik Bruhn. 220. *Nutcracker* (Pas de Deux; 1965). Erik Bruhn.

221

221. *Nutcracker* (Pas de Deux; 1965). Erik Bruhn, Anna Laerkesen. 222. *Don Quixote* (Pas de Deux; 1965). Erik Bruhn, Kirsten Simone. 223. *Romeo and Juliet* (1965). Kirsten Simone, Henning Kronstam.

224

225

224–227. Slavenska Franklin Ballet. 224. *A Streetcar Named Desire* (1953). Mia Slavenska, Frederic Franklin. 225. *A Streetcar Named Desire* (1952). Mia Slavenska.

128

226

227

226. *A Streetcar Named Desire* (1953). Valerie Bettis, Jamie Bauer. 227. *Mademoiselle Fifi* (1952). Roland Vazquez, Alexandra Danilova.

228

228. Helen Tamiris (1940s).

229–232. Paul Taylor Dance Company.
229. *Private Domain* (1969). Paul Taylor.

232

230. *From Sea to Shining Sea* (1969). Paul Taylor. 231. *Aureole* (1969).
Paul Taylor, Eileen Cropley. 232. *Aureole* (1969). Paul Taylor.

233

233, 234. Glen Tetley Dance Company. 233. *Pierrot Lunaire* (1969). Carmen de Lavallade, Glen Tetley. **234.** *Ricercare* (1969). Erin Martin, Scott Douglas.

Alphabetical List of Performers

The numbers are those of the illustrations.

Alphabetical List of Ballets and Dances

Titles beginning with a definite or indefinite article, in any language, are listed according to the word following. The numbers are those of the illustrations.